THE
TRANSCONTINENTAL
RAILROAD

👆 Workers pose in front of a Union Pacific construction train in 1868. The ambitious plan to connect America's East and West coast by rail could not have happened without dedicated laborers.

THE
TRANSCONTINENTAL
RAILROAD

JULIE RACH

MASON CREST PUBLISHERS

Mason Crest Publishers
370 Reed Road
Broomall PA 19008
www.masoncrest.com

Copyright © 2003 by Mason Crest Publishers.
All rights reserved. Printed and bound in the
Hashemite Kingdom of Jordan.

First printing

1 3 5 7 9 8 6 4 2

Library of Congress Cataloging-in-Publication Data
on file at the Library of Congress

ISBN 1-59084-063-1

Publisher's note: many of the quotations in this book come from
original sources, and contain the spelling and grammatical
inconsistencies of the original text.

CONTENTS

👆 After the last spike of the transcontinental railroad was driven into place, the Union and Central Pacific trains were christened with bottles of wine and champagne. Standing in the center of the action, Grenville Dodge and Samuel S. Montague shake hands.

A CROSS-COUNTRY DREAM

MAY 10, 1869, WAS A SPECIAL DAY ACROSS THE UNITED STATES. THE LIBERTY BELL rang. Soldiers fired cannon salutes from coast to coast. People gathered for parades and speeches.

One word started the celebrations: "Done." This simple message was sent by **telegraph** when the **transcontinental** railroad was finished. The telegraph wires were connected to a hammer that was used to pound in the last spike. The sound of the hammer blows were sent along the telegraph wires, too.

Work on the railroad had begun six years earlier in 1863 when two companies, the Central Pacific and the Union Pacific, began building the railroad across the country. The Central Pacific worked east from Sacramento, California, and the Union Pacific worked west from Omaha, Nebraska. When they met at Promontory Summit, Utah, the transcontinental railroad line was complete.

The cross-country railroad had been a dream for many people, one that had been talked about for years. As early as

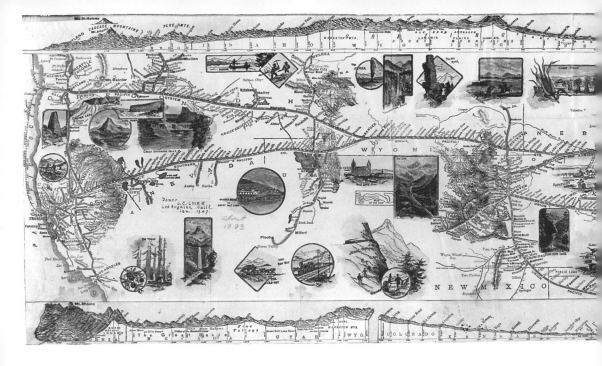

1817, people had demanded a railroad that would join the eastern states with the West Coast. At that time, no railroad tracks were laid anywhere in the United States, and they wouldn't be until 11 years later. However, some Americans had noticed what railroads were doing for England. These farseeing individuals recognized how much a huge nation like the United States would benefit from this new form of transportation. Many politicians even built their careers on the promise that the railroad would someday link the East and the West.

The railroad was needed to take settlers west. The long trip across country by covered wagon or stagecoach was slow, dusty, and bumpy—and sometimes even dangerous, given the number of bandits and outlaws that roamed the Wild West. Women were especially uncomfortable with stagecoach travel, since male travelers frequently used alcohol to help them wile away the long hours. Female passengers found themselves

> 🐟 The Union Pacific railroad connected the western states and made travel through them much easier and safer. This tourist map from 1893 shows the stops along the Union Pacific's route.

squashed into a corner of the stagecoach, forced to endure the loud voices and rude behavior of their masculine companions. They were understandably eager to find another option to stagecoach travel. Some people chose to travel west by ship, going south to the isthmus of Panama, crossing the narrow strip of land, and then continuing by ship up the continent's west coast—but this trip was also long and hard. A train trip was a far more convenient alternative.

The railroad would also take western products to eastern markets, which would help make western farms and ranches more profitable. Western minerals like gold and silver could be sent back east more quickly by train. A railroad would help America compete in world trading markets, too. Europe had long led the way in trade with Asian nations like China and Japan, but America wanted to trade with Asia, too. If products could come by ship directly from Asia to America's West Coast and be shipped from there to the East, then U.S. markets would no longer need to use Europe as a go-between. A transcontinental railroad could help make that dream come true.

Grenville Dodge (1831–1916) built Army railroads during the Civil War. His skill earned him the respect of many generals. The support of these men helped Dodge greatly when the time came for the Union Pacific to be built.

After the war, he became the chief engineer of the Union Pacific Railroad. Throughout his life, Dodge had many duties on the railroad. He wrote about it. He talked to officials in Washington about it. He ran operations from Omaha, directing the Union Pacific construction crews as they extended the tracks west.

When the transcontinental railroad was done, Dodge became engineer of another railroad in Texas. He helped set up routes across the country. He also helped build a railroad in Cuba. His last job in the army was as commander of the Department of the Missouri. One of the things he tried to do was keep the peace between the railroad and the Native Americans. Dodge also was a member of many veterans' organizations. He died in Iowa on January 3, 1916.

In 1853 Congress ordered **surveyors** to scout routes for the railroad. Five teams of men were sent out to explore routes across the country. One group studied the northern route, while two groups looked at central routes, and two other groups mapped southern routes. Over time, railroads were built along all these routes, but none of them was chosen for the first cross-country railroad.

☛ Jefferson Davis, a powerful politician from Mississippi, was a strong supporter of a southern route for the transcontinental railroad. In December 1860 Davis became president of the Confederate States of America—the organization of southern states that attempted to leave the United States after the election of Abraham Lincoln.

Congress looked at the surveys. The southern route seemed the best, because it crossed the fewest mountains and had the best weather all year long. But other issues in the country made this route less favorable. Among these was the question of slavery. People kept slaves in the South, while most people in the North believed everyone should be free. Neither side wanted the other to have a railroad through its states. Northern politicians would not support a southern rail route, and Southern politicians would not allow a northern route to be built. Discussions continued but no decisions were made; the country was locked in a stalemate.

Meanwhile, though, a man named Grenville Dodge had already begun to think about the best route for the cross-county railroad. He had surveyed much of Iowa and Nebraska

Abraham Lincoln (1809–1865) was the 16th president of the United States. Before becoming a politician, Lincoln was a lawyer. He often represented Illinois railroads, and he won many of their cases. He also helped set up railroad laws in several states.

In 1857, Lincoln worked for the Rock Island Bridge Company, which built the first railroad bridge over the Mississippi River. A boat owner sued the company after his boat crashed into the bridge. The boat owner said the bridge shouldn't have been built over the river, but Lincoln argued that the crash was caused by pilot error. Lincoln won the case.

Lincoln became president in 1860, at a time when the nation was split between North and South over the issue of slavery. The Civil War began a month after he took office. Although the war took much of his attention, Lincoln still found time for the railroad. He signed the Pacific Railroad Bill in July 1862. It created the Union Pacific Railroad. He also signed the Pacific Railroad Act of 1864. This law gave the railroads money to pay for construction.

Lincoln never got to see the transcontinental railroad completed, though. After the Civil War was over, Lincoln was shot and killed while he was watching a play.

for the Mississippi and Missouri Railroad, and now he was interested in the path for the transcontinental line.

In 1859, Dodge met Abraham Lincoln, a politician who would be elected president the next year. One of the things they talked about was the best route for a transcontinental railroad. Lincoln knew that Dodge had studied different routes for the railroad, and he asked Dodge which route he liked best. Dodge said that a route along the Platte River Valley made the most sense. This route would cross Nebraska and take the same path as the wagon road called the Mormon Trail. This alternative became known as the Great Platte Valley Route.

The Platte River flows through Nebraska, Iowa, and Missouri. It was an important waterway in the early West used by Native Americans and fur traders.

Omaha was at the eastern end of the Platte River Valley, and railroads already connected the city of Omaha to cities in the East. The valley was also pretty flat until it reached the Rocky Mountains. "The route was made by the buffalo, next used by the Indians," Dodge wrote later. "Then by the fur traders, next by the Mormons, and then by the overland immigration to California and Oregon."

The train route west would need many people to make it happen—surveyors, government officials, and workers. But most of all, the transcontinental railroad needed someone to direct and organize this huge venture, someone who could raise enough money to provide supplies and pay the surveyors and workers. A man named Theodore Judah dreamed of doing just that.

One of the most daunting tasks of building the railroad was blasting through the Sierra Nevada mountain range. This treacherous terrain was extremely dangerous to navigate.

THE CENTRAL PACIFIC

THEODORE JUDAH HAD COME TO
CALIFORNIA IN 1854 TO BUILD A
railroad near Sacramento, and he dreamed of
connecting California to the east. He dreamed
and talked about the railroad for more than five
years. People began to call him "Crazy Judah,"
because he talked about the Pacific railroad so
much. Most people thought the railroad was an
impossible dream. No single company could
afford to build the tracks across the country, and
nothing could be done without the government's
approval to pass over federal land. What's more,
the war between the North and South meant
that the existing **locomotives** would be needed in the east,
and few workers would be available to lay the line.

Judah visited Washington, D.C., three times in the late
1850s. He wanted the senators to pass a Pacific Railroad Bill,
but he found out that a route still hadn't been picked. The
senators argued about the route until the Civil War started in
1861. After the Southern senators left Washington in 1861, the

Northern senators chose Dodge's route. The route was named the Union Pacific because the politicians hoped it would help keep the Pacific states of California and Oregon with other Northern states in the Union.

Judah tried to raise money for his railroad in San Francisco. The wealthy people there didn't take his idea seriously, so he started talking about his idea in Sacramento. Some business

This political cartoon from the 1850s jokes about demands for a fast route west. It shows passengers on a tight string; when the string is cut, the passengers will fly off to the west. Within 20 years, however, the cross-country railroad, offering quicker travel to the west, had become a reality.

owners there began to listen to him. By 1861, Judah had found four men—Leland Stanford, Collis Huntington, Charles Crocker, and Mark Hopkins—who would pay for the railroad. These men became known as the Big Four.

Judah planned a route that would go east from Sacramento. It would have to cross the Sierra Nevada mountains, so Judah spent a lot of time finding the best route

Leland Stanford (1824–1893) was a lawyer and grocery store owner. He came to California during the gold rush. His knowledge of the law helped him settle arguments between the miners.

Stanford ran for state treasurer in 1857. He lost the race but found that he liked being in politics. He ran for governor in 1859 and lost. Stanford was part of the Republican Convention of 1860. This was the convention that nominated Abraham Lincoln for president.

Stanford was governor of California from 1861 to 1863. He was also president of the Central Pacific Railroad and president of the Southern Pacific Company. He ran ranches and a vineyard in northern California. Eventually, he became a U.S. Senator, too.

Stanford founded Leland Stanford Junior University in memory of his son, who died at age 15. He built the university on his favorite ranch at Palo Alto. He also picked the school's staff and helped develop its lesson plans.

He died at Palo Alto on June 21, 1893.

through the mountains. He made many surveying trips into the Sierra Nevadas, and he heard about a route over the Sierras through a town called Dutch Flat. This route was flatter than others that crossed the mountains. Judah went to see the Dutch Flat route and liked it.

A wagon road was built over the route first to help move supplies for the railroad. The wagon road was a **toll road**, too. The Big Four paid $350,000 to have it built. They owned it and collected tolls from miners and others who used the road.

The Sierra Nevadas are a mountain range between California and Nevada.

Judah arranged for supplies to be shipped west by boat. Nearly everything needed to build the railroad had to be sent from the East. This included the locomotives, railroad spikes, and even the rails themselves—but rails and locomotives were in short supply in the East because of the Civil War. **Black powder** needed for blasting tunnels was hard to find, too.

Charles Crocker (1822–1888) was in charge of construction for the Central Pacific Railroad. A member of the Big Four, his job title was general superintendent of the railroad. Under his leadership, the railroad was done seven years ahead of schedule.

Before he worked on the Pacific railroad, Crocker had a store in Sacramento where he sold cloth, thread, and carpet. Crocker was a member of the state legislature, too, but he gave up his business and his political career to build the railroad. After the railroad was built, Crocker helped build the Southern Pacific's rail route across the Southwest. He also built dams and helped develop California's Central Valley. He died on August 14, 1888.

The isthmus of Panama is the narrow strip of land that connects North America with South America. Today the Panama Canal cuts through this land, allowing ships to pass from the Atlantic into the Pacific Ocean.

Somehow, though, Judah managed to find the supplies he needed to start building the railroad.

Work began on the Central Pacific Railroad on January 8, 1863, in Sacramento. Leland Stanford, who had been elected governor of California, made a speech. He also turned over the first shovel of earth to break ground for the railroad. Other politicians spoke that day, too. They dreamed of how different life would be when California was connected to the East by the railroad.

Wet ground and winter rains delayed work on the railroad for a month. Charles Crocker ran the construction crews that started work in February 1863. They began to **grade** the **roadbed** east from Sacramento toward the mountains. The first contract called for the crews to build 18 miles of railroad track.

Judah soon began disagreeing with the Big Four. Some of the arguments were about building a headquarters for the Central Pacific Railroad. Judah wanted a fancy building he had designed. Instead, the Big Four put up a shack on the railroad's property. They continued to do railroad business in an office over Stanford's grocery store.

Collis Huntington (1821–1900) went to California during the Gold Rush. While he waited in Panama for the ship that would carry him up the west coast, he bought and sold things. He started with $1,200 and ended with $5,000. Once he reached California, he forgot about looking for gold; instead, he used his profit to start a hardware store in Sacramento. His partner in the store was Mark Hopkins, and their store was where Theodore Judah first explained his plan for the railroad to Huntington, Hopkins, Leland Stanford, and Charles Crocker—otherwise known as the Big Four.

Huntington was the vice president of the Central Pacific Railroad. One of his jobs was to sell bonds in New York, Washington, and other cities to help pay for the railroad. After the transcontinental railroad was built, he went on to buy other railroads, and he founded the town of Newport News, Virginia, as a port to which one of his railroads could send goods. Huntington died on August 13, 1900.

As time went on, Judah and the Big Four disagreed more often about how the railroad should be run. Sometimes they fought about how the Big Four were paying for the railroad construction. Other times they disagreed about the actual route of the tracks.

Mark Hopkins (1813–1878) was the Central Pacific Railroad's treasurer. Before he became Collis Huntington's partner, Hopkins had a store in Placerville during the Gold Rush. He was a lawyer, too.

The other members of the Big Four trusted Hopkins's judgment. They had him look over all their projects, and if he liked a project, the group went ahead with it. If he didn't, they backed out.

After the transcontinental railroad was done, Hopkins stayed in the railroad business. He worked for the Southern Pacific Railroad, and he died in Yuma, Arizona, on March 29, 1878, while inspecting the Sunset Route for that line.

In 1863, Judah went back East to discuss railroad operations with rich men there. Some people think he was trying to raise money to buy out the Big Four. However, after he sailed for New York, he caught **yellow fever** when he crossed the isthmus of Panama. He died after reaching New York.

Judah had been a man of principle, but the Big Four cared only about making money. They shared Judah's dream for a transcontinental railroad only because they knew the scheme could make them rich. But to get started, they had to use their own money. "We built the first 31 miles of road entirely from our own means," Leland Stanford said later. "We had not then obtained any county or state aid. We built 31 miles of road but we were not able to go on until we got county aid to go further."

The four men met to discuss the situation. They talked about what they had learned while building the first 31 miles. They found ways to cut costs. These included hiring only as many men as they could afford to pay at any given time. They put their money together and found a way to keep building. And they decided to ask the government for money.

By the end of the Civil War, there were thousands of miles of railroad tracks throughout the United States. However, most of these were in the northeastern and southern areas of the country. The transcontinental railroad was intended to link the west with the more settled areas of the east.

THE UNION PACIFIC

THE PACIFIC RAILROAD ACT OF 1862 GAVE GENEROUS GRANTS OF LAND TO the two railroads that would be built from the east and west to link the continent. The companies would receive a strip of land for the railroad line, as well as five sections of land on each side of the line. (Each section was 640 acres.) The railroad companies could help fund their construction by selling this land to settlers. The federal government also gave enormous low-interest loans to the railroads.

The Central Pacific Company, controlled by the Big Four, would build from the west. The U.S. government formed the Union Pacific Railroad Company to build from the east. A group of 163 commissioners met in Chicago to organize the company. The group hoped to sell **bonds** that would help pay for railroad construction. But with the Civil War going on, few people bought bonds.

In October 1863, permanent officers were chosen for the Union Pacific. John A. Dix was named president. He was also a

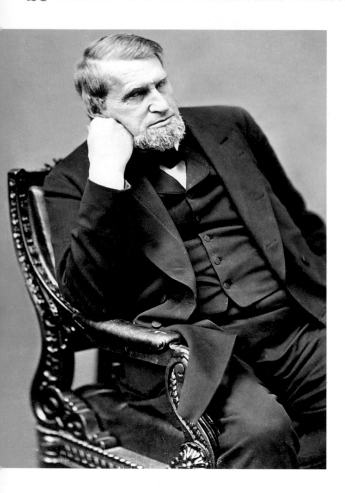

Oakes Ames, of the Oliver Ames & Sons business, was fortunate to amass a good deal of money during the California gold rush. When he and his brother, Oliver, undertook the financing of the Union Pacific railroad construction, they also bribed a congressman, leading to a scandal that tarnished their name.

general in the army, so he was too busy to run a railroad. The company's vice president, Thomas Durant, did most of the work. One of the first things Durant did was plan a party in Omaha. This party would celebrate the **groundbreaking** for the Union Pacific. The event took place December 1, 1863. The governor of the Nebraska Territory made a speech. Bands played. Fireworks and cannons were shot. The mayor of Omaha had a banquet and ball.

But parties and celebrations don't really accomplish much of anything practical. In the first year the Union Pacific operated, it did not lay a single **tie** or rail. All the company managed to do was grade 20 miles of roadbed west from Omaha.

Several things caused the delay. First was the lack of men to do the work. The Civil War was still being fought and many men were in the army. Durant himself caused other delays, though. He had purchased land in the area and wanted to make money by selling it once the railroad started running, so he wasted time surveying extra rail routes around Omaha. He also took time to form a company called the Credit Mobilier of America.

A man named Oakes Ames helped this company grow. Ames was a Massachusetts manufacturer of shovels, and he saw the railroad as a wonderful opportunity to sell his product. Ames and his brother Oliver backed the Union Pacific financially. Oakes Ames was a member of Congress and a member of the federal railroad committee, so he was in a good position to help the Union Pacific. When Durant came up with Credit Mobilier scheme, Oakes helped sell the idea to Congress.

The Credit Mobilier was actually a dummy company. The company received fat financial contracts from the government but the railroad itself never received this money. So as Durant, Ames, and the other members of the Credit Mobilier grew richer, the railroad fell deeper and deeper into debt. The Credit Mobilier also gave Union Pacific stock to Congressmen. These

Thomas C. Durant (1820–1885) was the vice president of the Union Pacific Railroad. The railroad president couldn't do his job because he was a general in the Civil War. So Durant took over the president's job.

Durant had studied medicine. He specialized in eye problems, but he didn't work long as a doctor. Instead, he worked for his uncle, exporting grain and flour. He also made money by investing in Wall Street. He was a man who valued wealth above all else, and he was involved in various dishonest money-making schemes.

Unfortunately for Durant, he lost most of his money in a financial panic in 1873. He died on October 5, 1885.

gifts bought them votes on bills that would help the railroad. Eventually, the truth would come out about the Credit Mobilier scheme, and the careers of the Ames brothers would be ruined by the scandal.

In the meantime, Durant continued to waste time and money as he speculated which route to take. He wanted to make sure that the railroad ran through the most desirable grants of land, so that homesteaders would be eager to buy up the territory. Durant cared far more about making a fortune than he did about running a railroad company.

At last, though, the American government pressured Durant into moving forward with the railroad construction. But now the lack of a chief engineer for the railroad caused another delay in the project. Durant wanted Grenville Dodge to be the Union Pacific's chief engineer. But Dodge had joined the Union Army to fight in the Civil War. He made it clear that he planned to stay in the army until the war was over.

While he was in the army, Dodge and his men built or rebuilt railroads throughout the South. The Union Army used these railroads to move troops and supplies. Dodge's skills at building railroads impressed his commander, General Ulysses S. Grant. When Grant was later president, he supported Dodge's efforts to build the Union Pacific Railroad.

At last, in April 1865, Dodge took a leave of absence from the army to go work for the railroad. He set up offices in Omaha and began to organize his work crews into an army of sorts. Many of the workers had served in the Union or Confederate armies during the Civil War, and they were used to orders and camp life.

Now serious construction could begin.

👆 Native Americans were angry when train tracks were laid through their lands. They often retaliated by attacking rail workers.

THE RACE BEGINS

THE UNION PACIFIC STARTED LAYING TRACK IN 1865. WORK SHOULD HAVE gone pretty fast because the plains of Nebraska are flat, so it is easy to lay track across them. But the crews only laid 40 miles of track that year.

Fights with Native Americans were one reason so little track was laid. The Cheyenne and Arapaho people were sick and hungry. Buffalo were hard to find, and so the tribes started attacking wagon trains to get food. They also raided stagecoach stations and ranches. And they attacked the railroad crews.

Another big reason the railroad got off to a slow start was that it was not run very well at first. After Dodge was hired, though, he organized the workers more efficiently. Two other good men, Jack and Dan Casement, were hired to head the construction crews.

Many of the workers were Civil War veterans looking for work. Many were also Irish laborers who had fled Ireland after the potato famines in the 1840s. Some of these men had

👆 William T. Sherman was a Union army general in the Civil War. A much-respected military man, his presence at the site of railroad labor brought public interest to the project.

helped build the Erie and the Illinois Central Railroads, and they knew how to work hard—but they also tended to be troublemakers when they weren't working. Without wives or families to calm them down, they were often a rowdy bunch. Whenever storms brought the work to a standstill, these mobs of men had to be housed in temporary "railroad towns" made up of crude shacks and tents. Keeping order in these settlements was a constant challenge to the crew leaders.

All in all, the railroad was an immense project. Durant wanted people to be interested in it, so he brought famous people like General William T. Sherman to Omaha to see the crews at work. Durant named the first locomotive engine on the Union Pacific line for the general, too. Ulysses S. Grant also visited the work crews when he was running for president. And Durant made sure that newspapers carried stories about the railroad construction.

One big story was when crews reached the 100th meridian, located about 250 miles west of Omaha. The tracks got to that point on October 5, 1866. Durant brought more than 200 important people there by special train to celebrate the crews' hard work. Reporters came along, too, to write about the trip. One reporter from the

The Cheyenne and Arapaho people were two Native American tribes that lived on lands crossed by the transcontinental railroad.

New York Times described North Platte, the noisy town that had sprouted up at the 100th meridian: "The larger part of the floating population is made up of desperados who spend their time in gambling of all kinds … Day and night the saloons are in full blast … astonishing to one who is not accustomed to the recklessness which their wild frontier life invariably begets."

By December 1866, the Union Pacific had laid 305 miles of track. More than 250 of those miles were built in the nine months between April and December, after the company finally got moving.

Meanwhile, the Central Pacific didn't make much progress for the first few years, either, but this company had a different set of problems. The Native Americans did not cause as much trouble for Central Pacific workers, because the Big Four tried to make friends with the Indians by giving them free passes on the trains as the line was being built.

But the land the Central Pacific worked on was not flat like that which the Union Pacific encountered. Central Pacific workers had to drill and blast tunnels through the Sierra Nevada Mountains. It took them three years to cross the mountains. (Today you can drive through the mountains from Sacramento to Reno in about two hours.)

The Central Pacific helped determine the official starting point of the Sierra Nevadas. Charles Crocker and state geologist Josiah Whitney went into the Sierra foothills to find

Brothers John (1829–1909) and Dan (1832–1881) Casement were in charge of laying track for the Union Pacific. John had joined the Union Army during the Civil War, while Dan stayed home to run their contracting business. John was a general by the end of the war, and his men sometimes called him "General Jack."

On the Union Pacific, John worked in the field, and Dan ran the business office. They organized their work crews into what was referred to as the Casement Army. The brothers also built special house cars with bedrooms, dining rooms, and kitchens. These cars followed the men down the track and gave them some of the comforts of home.

After the Union Pacific was done, the Casements kept building railroads in four other states, Canada, and Costa Rica. Dan died in 1881, John died in 1909.

where the mountains began. Whitney thought the start of the Sacramento River was the mountains' starting point, too—but Crocker wanted Whitney to say the mountains started about seven miles further west. He did this so the Central Pacific could collect more money, since government grants for rails laid through the mountains paid more than grants for track on flat land. Whitney agreed and the Central Pacific received an extra $240,000.

The Central Pacific also used a different set of workers from the Union Pacific. Charlie Crocker had an idea to get the Central Pacific Railroad built more quickly while spending less money. He decided to import workers from China.

A group of railroad workers prepare to start their day on the line. On April 28, 1869, a Union Pacific crew set a record by putting down more than 10 miles of track in a single day. They used 3,520 rails and more than 28,000 spikes.

WORKING ON THE RAILROAD

MANY MEN FOUND THEMSELVES WITHOUT
WORK AFTER THE CIVIL WAR. CONFEDERATE
soldiers moved west because they had little to go home to in
the South. Union soldiers went west, too, because the army
reduced its ranks after the war. Irish, Mexicans, Germans,
Italians, Native Americans, and African Americans also
provided the manpower needed to build the Union Pacific.

But manpower was a problem for the Central Pacific. Most
men who went to California were miners, not railroad
builders. The Central Pacific needed more than 10,000
workers, but at first they could only recruit about one-fifth of
that number. To make matters worse, many men were lured by
the get-rich-quick promise of gold and silver. These men quit
the railroad once the roadbed reached the mines in Nevada.

Charles Crocker suggested the company use Chinese
workers. People laughed at his idea, because many Americans
believed that Chinese were too frail and weak to do such hard
work. Crocker had worked with Chinese men on the Dutch
Flat wagon road, though, and he knew they were excellent
workers. Better yet, from Crocker's point of view, they were

willing to work for next to nothing, and they were far more law-abiding than many of the other workers.

So 50 Chinese men from northern California were tested on the railroad for a month. They worked out so well that soon the Central Pacific had hired most of the Chinese men in northern California, and many more came from China to work on the railroad. In less than a year, almost 4,000 Chinese men were working on the Central Pacific. They were paid only $30 to $35 a month; they caused their bosses no headaches; and they got along on meager supplies. From the perspective of the Central Pacific Company, they were the ideal workers.

But Chinese people were not always welcome in California. Some people didn't like them because they looked different; the Chinese railroad workers, in their blue pajamas, pigtails, and umbrella-shaped basket hats, stood out from the rest. Other people were jealous of the Chinese men's ability to work hard. These prejudices influenced the California government, who made the Chinese pay extra taxes to live there. The government hoped to discourage them from moving to California. They came anyway, though. Without the Chinese, the transcontinental railroad might never have been built.

A day in a railroad work camp followed a tight schedule. The men got up at first light. They ate breakfast and went to work. They worked until noon, when they took an hour for lunch. For the Union Pacific workers, lunch consisted of

One song sung by the Union Pacific workers was "Drill, Ye Tarriers, Drill." The lyrics tell about life on the railroad. The "tarriers" are Irish workers who dig for the railroad. The "tay" mentioned in the chorus is tea.

Every morning about seven o'clock
There were twenty tarriers drilling at the rock.
The boss comes along and he says, "Keep still
And bear down heavy on the cast iron drill. "

Chorus:
And drill, ye tarriers, drill.
Drill, ye tarriers, drill.
For it's work all day for the sugar in your tay
Down beyond the railway,
And drill, ye tarriers, drill,
And blast, and fire.

The foreman's name was John McCann.
By God, he was a blamed mean man.
Last week a premature blast went off,
And a mile in the air went big Jim Goff.

And when next payday came around,
Jim Goff a dollar short was found.
When he asked, "What for?" came this reply
"You were docked for the time you were up in the sky."

coffee, soup, fried meat, roast meat, potatoes, condensed milk, canned fruit, pies, and cakes. The Union Pacific brought a herd of cows with it as it moved west to provide beef for the crews.

The Chinese workers on the Central Pacific bought food with their own money. The other railroad workers spent much of their wages on alcohol and gambling, but the Chinese were far thriftier. Their diet included oysters, abalone, Oriental fruits, bamboo sprouts, seaweed, mushrooms, noodles, rice, and salted cabbage. Their healthier diet and lifestyle helped them be stronger workers.

After lunch, the laborers worked until almost dark. Then they ate supper and had a little time to relax before bed. In the evening, the men talked, played cards, and sang songs. The men worked Monday through Saturday from sunup to sundown.

The Chinese workers' routine was a little different. They washed themselves off at the end of each workday and changed their clothes. The non-Chinese workers, however, seldom took a bath more than once a week—if that. They didn't change clothes too often and may have worn the same clothes until they wore out.

The Chinese workers also boiled water to make the tea they drank each day. Boiling water kills germs that can make you sick, but the other workers drank water straight from streams or rivers. As a result, the Chinese workers were not sick as often as the other workers.

The railroad workers had specific jobs to do. The survey crews made sure that the railroad grade never rose steeper than 116 feet of rise per mile. The grading crews built the roadbed 20 miles at a time. They filled in ravines or flattened hills as needed to make the roadbed flat. The tracklayers set 2,500 railroad ties in place for each mile of track. Eight men placed the rails, four on each side of the track. Two men pulled the front end of the rail off the car, and the other men placed the back end of the rail on iron rollers. The men at the front of the rail ran 30 feet down the roadbed, where they dropped the rail in place. The men at the rear of the rail made sure the rail matched up with the last rail. The **gauge** of the rails was checked to make sure it was within the standard of four feet, eight and one-half inches between the rails. Iron spikes were dropped along the rails, and then the rail was fastened in place with 10 spikes that were pounded down with three hammer strokes each.

A rail could be held in place with a chair or a fishplate. A chair was an iron support for the rail that wasn't bolted to it, while a fishplate was a device that held the ends of two rails together. It was considered more permanent than a chair as a way to keep the rails together. Bolts were used to anchor the rails, too. A rail weighed 560 pounds and the crew could lay two pairs of rails a minute.

The crews lived alongside the rails. Some slept in tents and others lived in special railroad cars. They moved as the

The Lakota people were a Native American tribe that lived on lands crossed by the Union Pacific railroad.

railroads moved, working every day that the weather was good. The work crews shut down only when winter snows forced them to stop work for the year.

The Union Pacific work crews continued to face two big problems: the weather and the native tribes of the Plains. Winter weather meant that supplies could not be brought in from the East until late spring. The Cheyenne and Lakota tribes did not want the railroads on their lands, because the buffalo herds that provided food for these tribes would not cross the rails. Warriors from these tribes fought the work crews to keep them from laying track, but the workers fought back.

"Each [work] party would consist of 18 to 22 men, all armed," Dodge later wrote, "generally furnished with a military escort of from 10 men to a company under a competent officer. The duty of this escort was to protect the party when in camp. In the field, the escort usually occupied prominent hills…so as to head off sudden attacks by the Indians." Over time, the attacks decreased but they were a problem until the railroad was done.

The Union Pacific crews also had a problem finding the wood they needed for the line. Cottonwood, a soft wood that didn't make good railroad ties, was all they had to work with.

Bison often wandered onto the rail lines on the open plain. This posed a problem for the conductors of approaching trains, who solved the dilemma by firing upon the animals to scatter them.

The crews used a machine called a burnettizer to dry the ties. After the wood was dry, chemicals were injected into it, and then the tie was heated and dried again. This process made the ties usable, but they still rotted away faster than hardwood ties did.

The Central Pacific crews could cut trees for their ties from the slopes of the Sierra Nevada Mountains. But the Central Pacific continued to be slowed down by the rugged terrain. At first, the workers used black powder for blasting through the mountains. But this process soon seemed too slow for Charles Crocker and construction superintendent J. H. Strobridge.

"We are only averaging about one foot per day on each **face**," Crocker wrote in 1867, "and Stro and I have come to the conclusion that something must be done to hasten it. We are proposing to use **nitroglycerine**." This explosive was a fairly new invention.

Early shipments of nitroglycerine had exploded on ships and in San Francisco, and some people had been killed. The year before, the Central Pacific had decided to bring in the chemicals separately, then have a chemist make the nitroglycerine at the work site. As things turned out, though, workers were afraid of the explosive, and it had been put away as something too dangerous to use.

Now, however, the more powerful explosive was needed to get the tunnels done faster, and the Central Pacific leaders forced the workers to overcome their fears. Workers who used nitroglycerine did three times as much work as those who used black powder. Nitroglycerine was used on three tunnels through the Sierra Nevada Mountains.

But the winter snows also slowed the building of the railroad. "[The snow was] somewhere from 30 to 40 feet deep, as near as we could measure," Stanford said later. "The snow would fall sometimes five to six feet in the night; I believe in one case that nine feet fell in a single night. It obstructed all

In order to keep rail layers productive through the winter, snow sheds were built over the rails. These shelters protected the rail lines from harsh weather conditions, allowing the trains to continue running.

the roads, and made it almost impossible to get over the mountains." Stanford also recalled how the workers dug tunnels under the snow to reach the tunnels they were drilling through the mountains.

Such deep snowfall meant that the rails might be closed part of the year unless a way was found to keep the tracks

 Brigham Young led converted Mormons West in the 19th century. A prophet of the new church, he was also the founder of Salt Lake City, Utah.

clear. So the engineers began to build snow sheds in 1868 to cover the tracks. All together, about 37 miles of snow sheds had to be built through the Sierra Nevadas. These sheds used 65 million feet of wood and 900 tons of bolts and spikes. They were finished in 1869, but fire from the fuel used to power the trains sometimes damaged the sheds. Then they would have to be rebuilt. To counteract this danger, the railroad began sending out special water trains to keep the wooden sheds wet, reducing the risk of fire. Eventually, years later, the wooden sheds were replaced with concrete ones.

When work began on the transcontinental railroad, Salt Lake City was the biggest town between California and the eastern states. This city had been built by Mormons in 1846 when they moved west to practice their religion in freedom.

Brigham Young was the Mormons' leader. He wanted to be

part of the cross-country railroad, and so he offered advice on the area's weather and made suggestions about the route. By the time the work crews reached Utah, grasshoppers had eaten most of the Mormons' crops. The farmers were out of work and short on money. Young worked out a deal with the Union Pacific to provide workers for the railroad, and three of Young's sons were in charge of the construction

The Mormons were a religious group that built Salt Lake City. They came to the West to be able to practice their religion freely. The trail they followed as they moved from Iowa to Utah is called the Mormon Trail. It ran along the north bank of the Platte River.

crews. Fourteen hundred men were soon working on 54 miles of the railroad near Salt Lake City.

Young had hoped that the railroad would run through Salt Lake City, but the surveys showed that the route would have to run north of the city. Young was disappointed, but he eventually built a **spur line** from Ogden to Salt Lake City. Visitors soon began coming there regularly, and it became a thriving city.

But a lot of work still needed to be done on the transcontinental railroad.

6

THE END OF THE LINE

Pacific and Union Pacific would meet was not named. The
companies raced to see which one could lay the most track, but
no decision was made on the meeting point until April 1869.

Grenville Dodge and Collis Huntington met in Washington
on April 8 to decide the meeting point for the two railroads.
The meeting lasted all day and into the night. Finally, the
following day, the men reached an agreement: the two
railroads would meet at Promontory Summit in Utah, about 50
miles from the current end of each company's track. Congress
approved the location in a special night meeting and the
decision was finalized.

These golden memorial railroad spikes were used at
the meeting of the Union Pacific and Central Pacific
Railroads at Promontory, Utah. The connection of the rails
was one of the most significant moments for the United
States as a nation.

One woman took part in the Central Pacific's race to Promontory Summit. She was Hanna Maria Strobridge, wife of James Harvey Strobridge, the construction superintendent. She and their six children traveled in a special railroad car. She even brought her pet canary on the trip!

Meanwhile, the crews continued to work. Most of the work they did was done by hand. They had no bulldozers or jackhammers; no cars or buses to take them to and from work; and no dump trucks to help haul away the dirt.

One day's work by the Central Pacific crews is still a marvel of construction. On April 28, 1869, a Central Pacific crew laid 10 miles and 56 feet of track in Utah. No one before or since has laid that much track in one day.

Charles Crocker and the Central Pacific crews planned their day carefully. Rail cars were carefully loaded with supplies and men. The first cars were brought to the end of the line and unloaded in just eight minutes. The men went to work as the cars went back for more supplies and men—850 men in all. Supplies followed the workers along the track all day long, so that the men could do the most work possible that day. They didn't waste time looking for supplies or waiting for things to be brought to them.

The crews started at 7 A.M., and they had laid six miles of

track by lunchtime. After lunch, the route they worked on had more curves. This meant the eight tracklayers lost time as they bent the rails to fit the route.

When the crews stopped working at 7 P.M., the eight tracklayers had lifted more than 125 tons of iron. They laid almost a mile of track every hour that day, and more than 3,500 rails were put down. Almost 26,000 ties were put in place, while more than 28,000 spikes and 14,000 bolts were used to hold the rails and ties in place.

The city of Sacramento gave the crew a parade a few days after their record-setting workday. The railroad paid each of the eight tracklayers four days' wages for their hard work. Now they were that much closer to the end of their goal.

Soon, the Central Pacific and Union Pacific were close enough to one another that they began to duplicate work. The two companies built more than 200 miles of parallel grades before Congress stepped in and stopped the work.

The builders wanted to celebrate the end of the railroad with a special event. They decided to connect the two railroads with a golden spike that would represent California. The Golden Spike ceremony was supposed to happen May 8, 1869, but the train carrying Union Pacific officials was delayed when rains damaged a bridge. So the ceremony took place May 10.

Parties were held across the country, while Leland Stanford and Grenville Dodge made speeches at Promontory Summit.

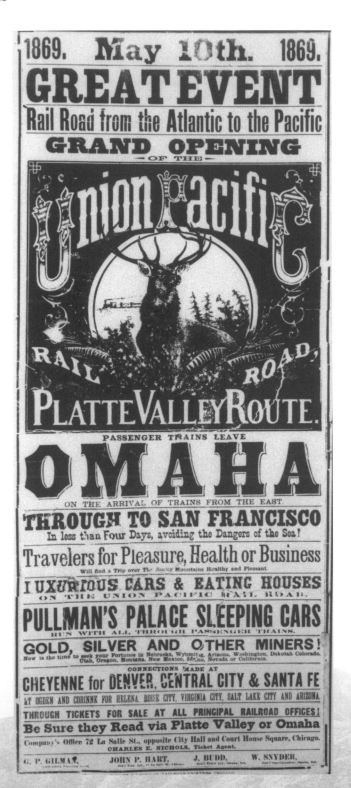

The golden spike was presented and hammered home. Photographers took pictures of two railroad engines meeting from the east and west. In the photographs, the Central Pacific's engine Jupiter is on the left of the picture. The Jupiter used wood for fuel and had a round, covered smokestack. On the right is the Union Pacific's engine 119. The 119 burned coal and had a straight

Four spikes were hammered into the final tie by Thomas Durant and Leland Stanford—two made of gold, one silver, and one a composite of silver, gold, and iron. The golden spike was engraved with a prayer: "May God continue the unity of our Country as this Railroad unites the two great Oceans of the world."

smokestack. The crews gathered around the engines to shake hands and drink toasts to the end of the railroad.

The golden spike representing California was not the only one used. A silver spike from Nevada and a gold, silver, and iron spike from Arizona were used, too. The ceremony also used a special laurel tie as the last tie in the railroad. A regular tie replaced it after the ceremony, but the crowd whittled the

The opening of the Union Pacific railroad revolutionized the settling of the West. Travel was now more economical and efficient than ever before.

replacement into souvenir splinters. Another tie was put in place, and again the crowd destroyed it and several more for souvenirs. The golden spike was saved after the ceremony. It went on display at Stanford University.

The Pacific railroad now stretched 1,776 miles from Omaha to Sacramento. The Union Pacific crews had laid 1,086 miles of track, and the Central Pacific crews had put down 690 miles. Travelers could now cross the country in a week for less than $100, compared to the months long, thousand-dollar trip by sea or stagecoach.

The Union Pacific-Central Pacific route would not be the only rail route across the country for long. By 1872— three years after the transcontinental railroad was completed—three other railroads across the country had been started. And by January 6, 1893, when the last spike was driven into the Great Northern's railway, five railroad

By the start of the 20th century, travelers to the West could use one of 10 railroads to get where they were going. The Great Northern's route that traveled between St. Paul and Seattle was the most northern route, while the southernmost route, connecting New Orleans and Los Angeles, belonged to the Southern Pacific. The others were large regional lines that connected the cross-country routes.

systems—the Union Pacific, Southern Pacific (which had merged with the Central Pacific in 1885), Santa Fe, Northern Pacific, and Great Northern—spanned the West. Their railroads followed the general routes of the original railroad surveys done during the 1850s. During the 1880s, approximately 40,000 miles of track were added to the railroads in the West.

You can still visit the site where the railroads met in 1869. The National Park Service runs the Golden Spike National Historic Site near Brigham City, Utah. Visitors can walk around replicas of the 119 and the Jupiter engines or can watch movies and hear talks by rangers. They can see where 10 miles of track were laid in one day. A reenactment of the Golden Spike ceremony takes place each May to celebrate an enormous achievement—the construction of the transcontinental railroad.

GLOSSARY

Black powder
Explosive powder used to blast tunnels on the Central Pacific Railroad.

Bond
A certificate issued by the government or a company promising to pay back borrowed money at a fixed rate of interest on a specified date.

Face
An exposed rock surface.

Gauge
Distance between the rails of a railroad.

Grade
To make a surface level.

Groundbreaking
An event that celebrates the start of a new project.

Locomotives
Self-propelled vehicles that run on rails and move railroad cars

Nitroglycerine
An oily and powerful explosive liquid.

Roadbed
Where the ties and rails of the railroad rest.

Spur line
A railroad track that branches off a main route.

Surveyor
A person who measures and maps the land.

Telegraph
A way to communicate over wire using a series of dots and dashes to represent the alphabet.

Tie

The wooden part of the railroad that the rails lie on. The rails are spiked to the ties to keep them straight.

Toll road

A private road that the owners collect a fee (or toll) from users.

Transcontinental

Across a continent.

Yellow fever

A disease caused by the bite of a yellow-fever mosquito. The last case in the United States was reported in the early 1940s.

TIMELINE

1853

Congress authorizes surveys for a transcontinental railroad.

1854

Army Corps of Engineers surveys transcontinental railroad routes.

Theodore Judah becomes engineer for the Sacramento Valley Railroad in California.

1856

Judah discusses a transcontinental railroad in Washington, D. C.

1859

Abraham Lincoln and Grenville Dodge talk about a railroad route on August 13.

1861

Civil War starts on April 12.

Central Pacific Railroad of California forms on June 28.

1862

President Lincoln signs Railroad Act of 1862 on July 1, forming the Union Pacific Railroad Company.

1863

Work starts January 8 on the Central Pacific Railroad.

Theodore Judah dies of yellow fever on November 2.

Work starts December 1 on the Union Pacific Railroad.

1865

The Civil War ends on April 9.

Abraham Lincoln is assassinated on April 15, and Andrew Johnson becomes president.

1867-1868

Forty feet of snow falls in the Sierra Nevada Mountains during the winter, slowing work on the Central Pacific Railroad.

1869

Meeting point for the Central Pacific and Union Pacific lines is chosen April 9. The rails will meet at Promontory Summit, Utah.

Central Pacific crews lay 10 miles and fifty-six feet of track in one day on April 28.

The rails of the Central Pacific and the Union Pacific meet May 10 at Promontory Summit, Utah.

FURTHER READING

Ambrose, Stephen. *Nothing Like It In the World: The Men Who Built the Transcontinental Railroad 1863–1869*. New York: Simon and Schuster, 2000.

Bain, David. *Empire Express: Building the First Transcontinental Railroad*. New York: Viking, 1999.

Cahill, Marie, and Lynne Piade. *The History of the Union Pacific: America's First Transcontinental Railroad*. New York: Crescent Books, 1989.

Durbin, William. *The Journal of Sean Sullivan: A Transcontinental Railroad Worker*. New York: Scholastic, 1999.

Fraser, Mary Ann. *Ten Mile Day and the Building of the Transcontinental Railroad*. New York: Henry Holt Publishers, 1996.

Gregory, Kristiana. *The Great Railroad Race: The Diary of Libby West*. New York: Scholastic, 1999.

Kalman, Bobbie. *The Railroad*. New York: Crabtree Publishing, 1999.

Krensky, Stephen. *The Iron Dragon Never Sleeps*. New York: Bantam Dell Doubleday Books for Young Readers, 1994.

Ward, Geoffrey. *The West: An Illustrated History*. Boston: Little, Brown and Company, 1996.

Williams, John. *A Great and Shining Road: The Epic Story of the First Transcontinental Railroad*. New York: Times Books, 1988.

INTERNET RESOURCES

Information about the Transcontinental Railroad
www.nps.gov/gosp
www.cprr.com/faster.html
www.uprr.com/uprr/ffh/history
www.csrmf.org/transbuild.html

Railroads of the West
http://homepage.interaccess.com/~dreyfus/history.html
http://www.americanwest.com/
http://web.uccs.edu/~history/index/west.html

Leland Stanford
http://www.pbs.org/weta/thewest/people/s_z/stanford.htm
http://www.sfmuseum.org/bio/stanford.html
http://www.usdreams.com/Stanford10.html

Collis Huntington
http://www.newrivertrain.com/

INDEX

PHOTO CREDITS

2:        Hulton/Archive
6–7:   National Archives
8–9:   Hulton/Archive
10:       Denver Public Library
11:       National Archives
12:       National Archives
14–15:   Roger Ressmeyer/Corbis
16:       Hulton/Archive
18:       Hulton/Archive
21:       Bettmann/Corbis
22:       Hulton/Archive
24–25:   Hulton/Archive
26:       Hulton/Archive

28:       Bettmann/Corbis
30–31:   Hulton/Archive
32:       Hulton/Archive
36–37:   Hulton/Archive
43:       Hulton/Archive
45:       Denver Public Library
46:       Hulton/Archive
48:       James L. Amos/Corbis
52:       Bettmann/Corbis

Cover photos:
(front) National Archives
(back)   Hulton/Archive

ABOUT THE AUTHOR

Julie Rach has been interested in the Pacific Railroad for many years. She is a lifelong student of western American history. She has also written 10 books about pets. She lives in Oceanside, California.